Crazy
Cats

Other Books by Bob Walker and Frances Mooney

The Cats' House

Cats into Everything

Comical Cats

Crazy Cats

Bob Walker and Frances Mooney

**Andrews McMeel
Publishing**

Kansas City

Crazy Cats

00 01 02 03 04 TWP 10 9 8 7 6 5 4 3 2 1

Library of Congress Cataloging-in-Publication Data
Walker, Bob.
  Crazy cats / Bob Walker and Frances Mooney.
       p. cm.
  ISBN 0-7407-1026-5
       1. Cats—Pictorial works. 2. Photography of cats. I. Mooney, Frances. II. Title.

SF446.W26 2000
636.8'0022'2—dc21   00-029944

www.catshouse.com

Book design by Holly Camerlinck

Attention: Schools and Businesses

Andrews McMeel books are available at quantity discounts with bulk purchase for
educational, business, or sales promotional use. For more information, please write to:
Special Sales Department, Andrews McMeel Publishing, 4520 Main Street,
Kansas City, Missouri 64111.

Acknowledgments

Without the fur and purr, we wouldn't be the cataholics that we are today. Thank you to the following for enriching our lives in ways that we could never have imagined: Sissypoo, George, Edward, Little Kitty, Harry, Gina, Herman, Alexander, Cornelius, Mr. Pie, Betsy, Dink, Lydia, Elizabeth, Emma, Virginia, Julia, BoyCat, Athena, Miranda, Snoopy, Beauregard, Benjamin, Calafia, Simon, Joseph, TomCat, Terri, Celeste, Jerry, Jimmy, Bernard, Denise, Frank, Molly, Louise, Charlotte, Gus, Elliott, all our future feline friends whose names will be revealed when the timing is right, and, of course, loving Sasha, the most catlike dog that could have found us.

There have also been several two-leggeds who've doggedly made *Crazy Cats* possible: Kathy Viele, our super editor and spokescat to our Andrews McMeel Publishing family—Tom Thornton, HughCat Andrews, Jim Andrews, Jan Girando, Patrick Regan, Heather Stewart, Kevin Worley, Eden Thorne, John Carroll, Tim Lynch, Michelle Daniel, Holly Camerlinck, and Norman Rockwell's likely niece, Katie Mace; Laurie and Chloe Fox, our confidants and inspiration at Linda Chester Literary Agency; lifelong supporters Gerri Calore and Denise Johnston and their wonderful staff at the National Cat Protection Society; Dr. Harold Stephens, Dr. Cheryl Clark, Jessica Dettweiler, Kimberlee Miskovsky, and

Charmain Sanchez at Fletcher Hills Pet Clinic, who keep our family fit for print; Dennis and Sue Reiter, Tim Bee, and Sam Nakamura at Chrome Film and Digital Services; Amy Shojai at the Cat Writers' Association; Lee Austin; John Bergstreser; Kay and Margie Crosbie; Tim, Sherry, and Thumper Crump; Dennis, Barbara, Christine, Andrew, and Jenny Culleton; Omer Divers and Katherine Mooney; Dave Garcia; Louis Goldich; John and Laura Cunningham-Hilbig; Melinda Holden; Naomi Kartin; Mary Beth Link and Norman Sizemore; Patrick Miller; Wayne and Nora Miller; Barbara Murray; Pat Rose; Brian and Carrie Soler; Jan, Linda, and Puddy Tonnesen; Karen Truax; Hitoshi, Terri, Ken, Issey, Ralphie, and Yohji Tsuchida; and our never-to-be-forgotten cat mom and poetic muse, Stelle Mooney.

Crazy Cats

Everyone who loves cats knows that felines are pretty crazy critters. They'll be purring in the sunshine one minute and climbing the drapes the next. They can transform a simple paper sack into a crinkly, crackly toy, and be totally bored by the new "all cats love" toy. They can be impossible to catch for their vet appointments, and impossible to ignore when you are trying to nap. They can gracefully stroll along a narrow tree limb and clumsily slip on a wooden floor. Cats are funny, wild, moody, unpredictable, and downright crazy . . .

because they

grin

because they **fluff**

because they put their

best Whiskers forward

because they are born magicians

because temptation always gets the best of them

because they are
willing to be
strung along

because they share their spoils

because they are

underfoot

because they
need
to be with us

because they hide

in plain sight

because they purr

because they make their feelings known

because they are fur balls

because they surprise us

because they make

fUNnY faces

because they are into everything

because they are there for us

because they trust

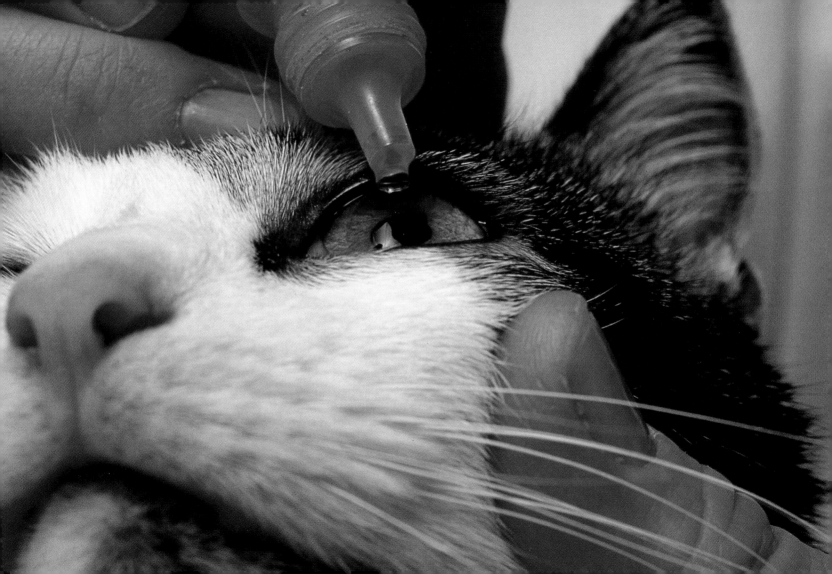

because they
play upon
our sympathy

because they have

opinions

because they know they are
superior

Light and Film

The Print

Color

The Studio

Photography As a Tool

Frontiers of Photography

Photojournalism

The Great Themes

Travel Photography

The Art of Photography

Special Problems

Documentary Photography

Photographing Children

Great Photographers

Photographing Nature

Caring for Photographs / Display Storage Restoration

PHOTOGRAPHY YEAR / 1973 EDITION

PHOTOGRAPHY YEAR / 1974 EDITION

PHOTOGRAPHY YEAR / 1975 EDITION

PHOTOGRAPHY YEAR / 1976 EDITION

PHOTOGRAPHY YEAR / 1977 EDITION

LIFE LIBRARY

because they go

wherever

they want

because they look up to us

because they are not so

independent

because they revel in a good scratch

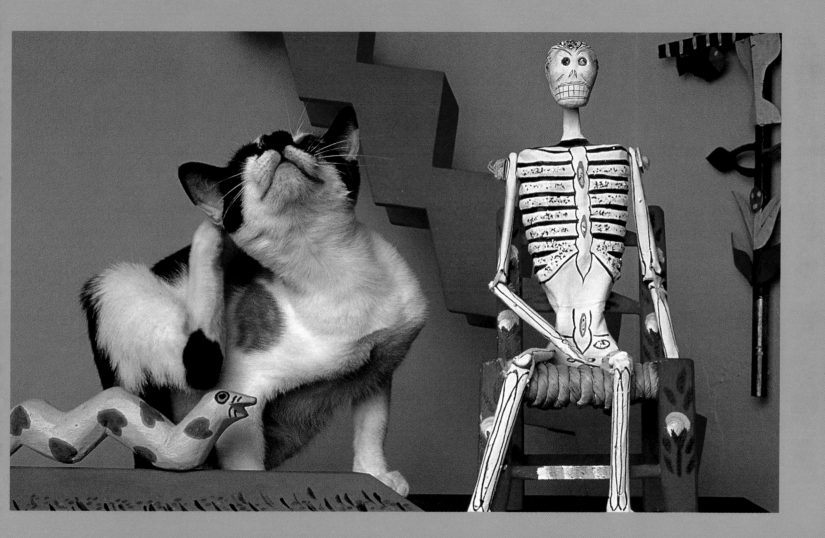

because they are

supple

because they

streeeeeeeeetch

because they are
sneaky

because
they are
alert

because they are

aVid
bird watchers

because they are

Scaredy-
Cats

because they are

hydrophobic

because they are
self-cleaning

because they look forward
to better days

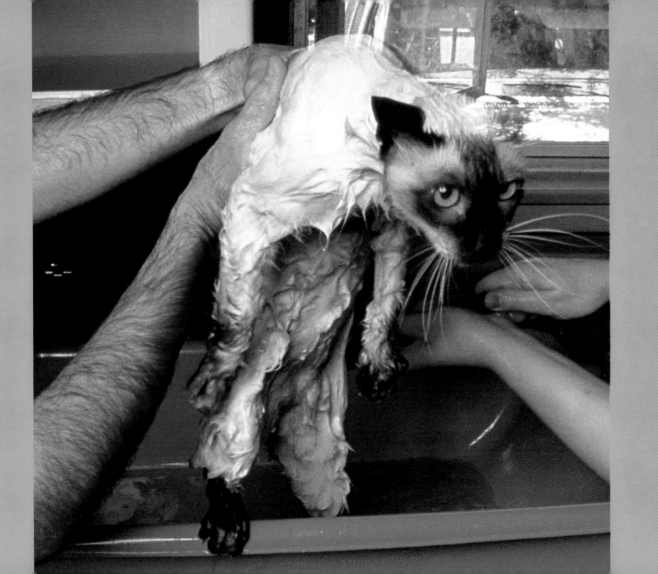

because they flaunt their freedom

because they welcome
new
arrivals

because they are

the best of friends

because they give
love nips

because they grow
old
and wise

because they are
self-sufficient

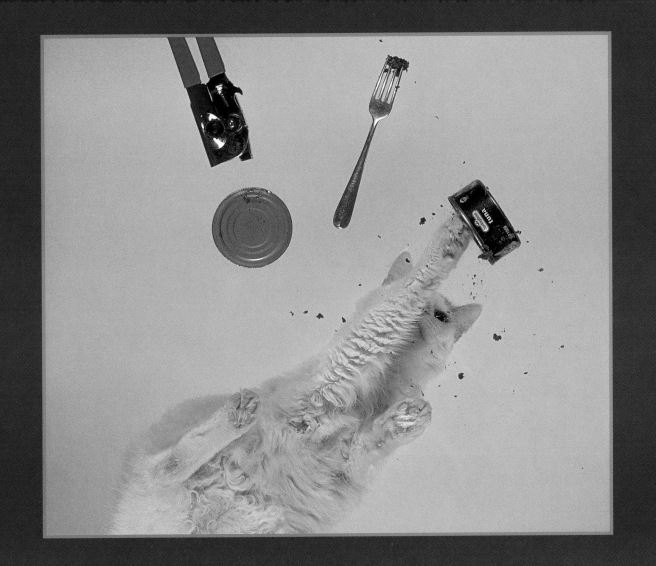

because they appreciate
fine dining

because they

stalk

because they
are stealthy

because they know a

good thing

when they see it

because they don't cry over

spilled milk

because they are
gluttons

because they bite the hand that feeds them

because they are
hungry to the last
crunch

because they love
our
attention

because they have their
limits

because they
play
tough

because they make
their own
toys

because they have a ball

because they are

fleet-footed

because they are surprised by unexpected pleasures

because they are

playful

because they stand up for themselves

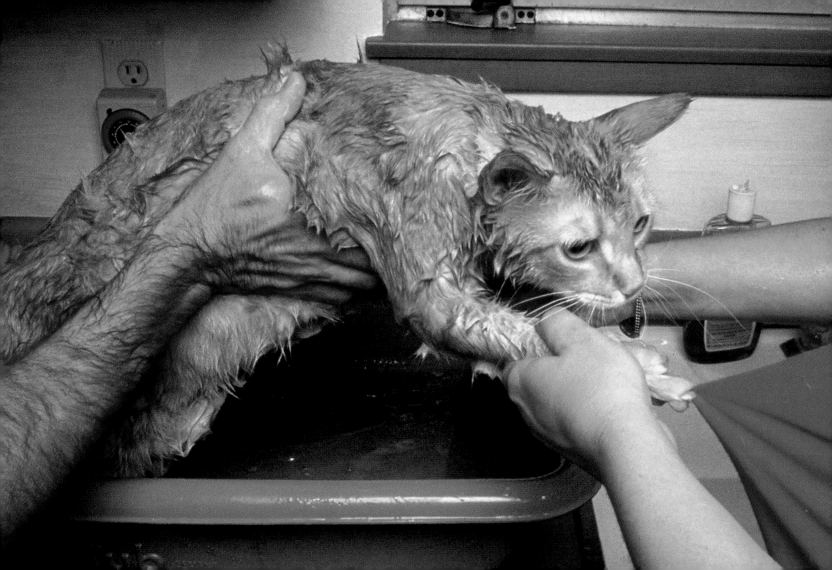

because they find
entertainment
everywhere

because they are
skillful

because they are
thrill
seekers

because they get themselves into trouble

because they are
curious

because they
love
helping

because they purr
when pressed into
service

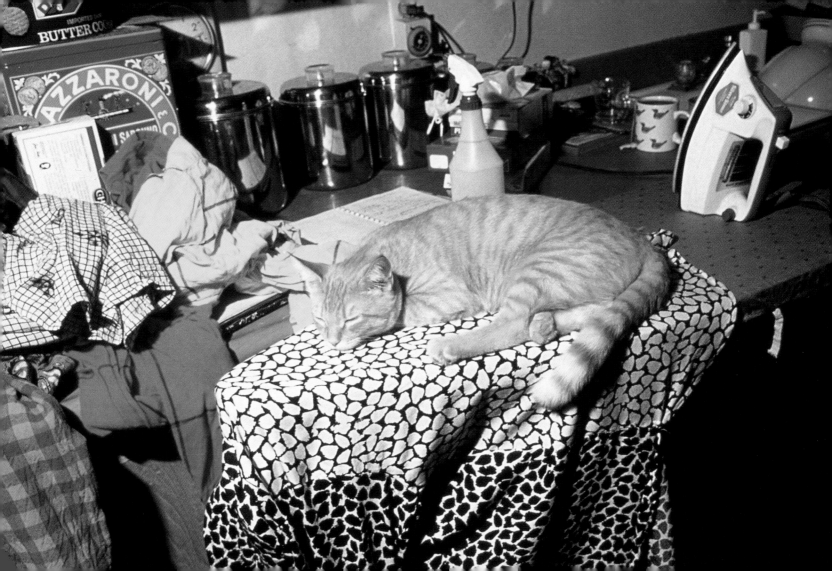

because they are
well designed

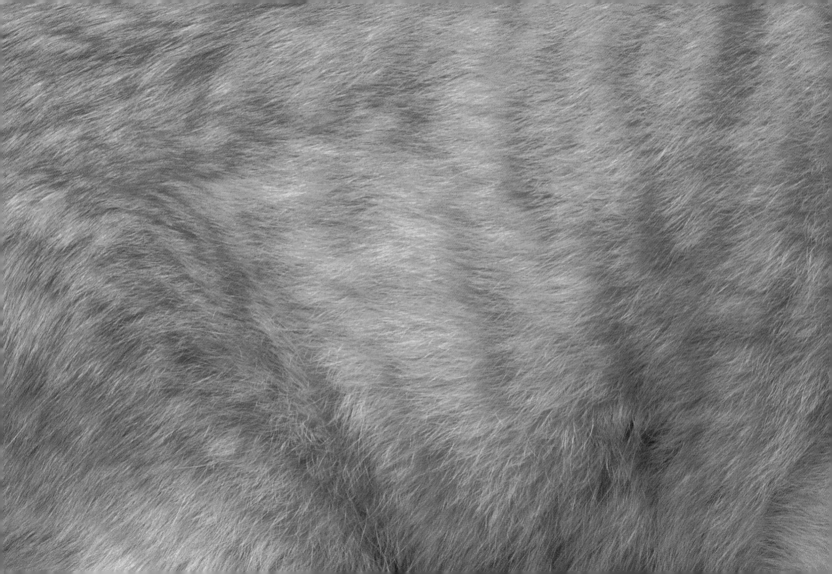

because they look good
at all angles

because they don't have
perfect
figures

because they are
fashion
victims

because they are striped
to the tips
of their tails

because they are charming

in all

positions

because they mug
for the camera

because they are *curly*

when wet

because they are
pensive

because they will sleep

anywhere

because they are

bed buddies